THE CHAPLET OF
SAINT MICHAEL THE ARCHANGEL
IN LATIN AND ENGLISH

THE CHAPLET OF
SAINT MICHAEL THE ARCHANGEL
IN LATIN AND ENGLISH

Edited by
Geoffrey W.M.P. Lopes da Silva

DOMINA NOSTRA PUBLISHING
Monterey, California, USA

Published in 2021 by
Domina Nostra Publishing
P.O. Box 1464, Monterey, CA. 93942-1464 USA
Email: info@DominaNostraPublishing.com
Website: www.DominaNostraPublishing.com

Copyright © 2021 Domina Nostra Publishing

Printed and bound in the United States of America.
All rights reserved.

The Raccolta: Prayers and Devotions Enriched with Indulgences (Benziger Brothers Inc., 1957).

The Revised Standard Version of the Bible: Catholic Edition (Division of Christian Education of the National Council of the Churches of Christ in the United States of America, 1965, 1966).

Although the editor and publisher have made every effort to ensure the accuracy and completeness of information contained in this book, we assume no responsibility for errors, inaccuracies, omissions, or any inconsistency herein. Any slights of people, places, or organizations are unintentional, and will be corrected in the next edition.

First printing, 2021.

ISBN: 978-0-9741900-1-3

"For He will give His angels charge of you
to guard you in all your ways.
On their hands they will bear you up,
lest you dash your foot against a stone".

Psalm 90 (91):11-12

*« Quoniam angelis suis mandabit de te,
ut custodiant te in omnibus viis tuis.
In manibus portabunt te,
ne forte offendas ad lapidem pedem tuum ».*

Psalmus 90 (91), 11-12

Introduction

In 1751, Saint Michael the Archangel appeared to the Servant of God Antonia d'Astonac, a Carmelite nun in Portugal. Saint Michael told her that he wished to be honoured by nine salutations corresponding to the nine Choirs of Angels. This should consist of one Our Father and three Hail Marys in honour of each of the angelic choirs.

It is said that those who would practice this devotion would have, when approaching Holy Communion, an escort of nine angels chosen from each one of the nine choirs of angels. In addition, for the daily recital of these nine salutations, Saint Michael promised his continual assistance and that of all the holy angels during life, and after death, deliverance from purgatory for themselves and their relations.

This private revelation to the Servant of God Antonia d'Astonac and the Chaplet of Saint Michael (Angelic Chaplet) was approved by Blessed Pius IX by a decree of the Sacred Congregation of Rites (*Sacrorum Rituum*) on 8 August 1851.

Various prayers (*orationes variae*) to Saint Michael the Archangel and the Holy Angels have also been included in this volume.

Corona Sancti Michaelis Archangeli
vel Corona angelica

ACTUS CONTRITIONIS

Deus meus, ex toto corde pǽnitet me
ómnium meórum peccatórum,
éaque detéstor, quia peccándo,
non solum pœnas
a te iuste statútas proméritus sum,
sed præsértim quia offéndi te,
summum bonum,
ac dignum qui super ómnia diligáris.
Ídeo fírmiter propóno,
adiuvánte grátia tua,
de cétero me non peccatúrum
peccandíque occasiónes próximas fugitúrum.
Amen.

℣. Deus, ✠ in adiutórium meum inténde.
℟. Dómine, ad adiuvándum me festína.

℣. Glória Patri, et Fílio,
et Spirítui Sancto.
℟. Sicut erat in princípio, et nunc et semper,
et in sǽcula sæculórum. Amen.

SALUTATIO I

Per intercessiónem Sancti Michǽlis
et cappéllæ cæléstis Séraphim,
Dóminus nos dignos
effíciat incéndi igne caritátis perféctæ. Amen.

℣. PATER NOSTER, qui es in cælis:
sanctificétur nomen tuum;
advéniat regnum tuum;
fiat volúntas tua,
sicut in cælo, et in terra.

The Chaplet of Saint Michael the Archangel
or The Angelic Chaplet

ACT OF CONTRITION

O my God, I am heartily sorry
for having offended You,
and I detest all my sins,
because I dread the loss of heaven,
and the pains of hell;
but most of all because they offend You, my God,
who are all good
and deserving of all my love.
I firmly resolve,
with the help of Your grace,
to sin no more
and to avoid the near occasions of sin.
Amen.

℣. O God, ✠ come to my assistance.
℟. O Lord, make haste to help me.

℣. Glory to the Father, and to the Son,
and to the Holy Spirit.
℟. As it was in the beginning, is now,
and will be for ever. Amen.

SALUTATION I

By the intercession of Saint Michael
and the Celestial choir of Seraphim,
may the Lord make us worthy
to burn with the fire of perfect charity. Amen.

℣. OUR FATHER, who art in heaven,
hallowed be thy name;
thy kingdom come,
thy will be done
on earth as it is in heaven.

℟. Panem nostrum cotidiánum da nobis hódie;
et dimítte nobis débita nostra,
sicut et nos dimíttimus debitóribus nostris;
et ne nos indúcas in tentatiónem;
sed líbera nos a malo. Amen.

Ters:

℣. Ave, María, grátia plena,
Dóminus tecum.
Benedícta tu in muliéribus,
et benedíctus fructus ventris tui, Iesus.

℟. Sancta María, mater Dei,
ora pro nobis peccatóribus,
nunc et in hora mortis nostræ. Amen.

Salutatio II

Per intercessiónem Sancti Michǽlis
et cappéllæ cæléstis Chérubim,
Dóminus nobis grátiam
det relínquere vias malas
et continuáre in vias perfectiónis Christiánæ. Amen.

Pater noster… Ters: Ave María…

Salutatio III

Per intercessiónem Sancti Michǽlis
et cappéllæ cæléstis Thronórum,
infúndat Dóminus in córdibus nostris
spíritum sincérum vérumque humilitátis. Amen.

Pater noster… Ters: Ave María…

The Chaplet of St Michael the Archangel

℟. Give us this day our daily bread,
and forgive us our trespasses,
as we forgive those who trespass against us;
and lead us not into temptation,
but deliver us from evil. Amen.

Three times:

℣. HAIL, MARY, full of grace,
the Lord is with you;
blessed are you among women,
and blessed is the fruit of your womb, Jesus.

℟. Holy Mary, Mother of God,
pray for us sinners
now and at the hour of our death. Amen.

SALUTATION II

By the intercession of Saint Michael
and the Celestial choir of Cherubim,
may the Lord vouchsafe to grant us grace
to leave the ways of wickedness
and run in the paths of Christian perfection. Amen.

Our Father… Three times: Hail Mary…

SALUTATION III

By the intercession of Saint Michael
and the Celestial choir of Thrones,
may the Lord infuse into our hearts
a true and sincere spirit of humility. Amen.

Our Father… Three times: Hail Mary…

Salutatio IV

Per intercessiónem Sancti Micháelis
et cappéllæ cæléstis Dominatiónum,
Dóminus nobis grátiam det gubernáre sensus
et domináre carnem petulantíssimam. Amen.

Pater noster… Ters: Ave María…

Salutatio V

Per intercessiónem Sancti Micháelis
et cappéllæ cæléstis Potestátum,
Dóminus ánimas nostras deféndat
contra tentatiónes et insídias diáboli. Amen.

Pater noster… Ters: Ave María…

Salutatio VI

Per intercessiónem Sancti Micháelis
et cappéllæ cæléstis Virtútum,
Dóminus nos servet a malo
et non permíttat cádere in tentatiónem. Amen.

Pater noster… Ters: Ave María…

Salutatio VII

Per intercessiónem Sancti Micháelis
et cappéllæ cæléstis Principatórum,
Dóminus ánimas nostras
spíritu vero obœdiéntiæ ímpleat. Amen.

Pater noster… Ters: Ave María…

SALUTATION IV

By the intercession of Saint Michael
and the Celestial choir of Dominions,
may the Lord give us grace to govern our senses
and subdue our unruly passions. Amen.

Our Father… Three times: Hail Mary…

SALUTATION V

By the intercession of Saint Michael
and the Celestial choir of Powers,
may the Lord vouchsafe to protect our souls
against the snares and temptations of the devil. Amen.

Our Father… Three times: Hail Mary…

SALUTATION VI

By the intercession of Saint Michael
and the Celestial choir of Virtues,
may the Lord preserve us from evil,
and suffer us not to fall into temptation. Amen.

Our Father… Three times: Hail Mary…

SALUTATION VII

By the intercession of Saint Michael
and the Celestial choir of Principalities,
may God fill our souls
with a true spirit of obedience. Amen.

Our Father… Three times: Hail Mary…

Salutatio VIII

Per intercessiónem Sancti Michǽlis
et cappéllæ cæléstisis Archangelórum,
Dóminus nobis constántiam in fide
   et opéribus bonis det,
ut glóriam Paradísi obtineámus. Amen.

Pater noster… Ters: Ave María…

Salutatio IX

Per intercessiónem Sancti Michǽlis
et cappéllæ cæléstis Angelórum,
Dóminus ab eis protegémur
   in hac vita mortále det
et posthac perdúci ad glóriam ætérnam. Amen.

Pater noster… Ters: Ave María…

Conclusio

In honóro Michǽlis: Pater noster…

In honóro Gabriélis: Pater noster…

In honóro Raphǽlis: Pater noster…

In honóro angelus custos: Pater noster…

Antiphona

O Princeps glorióse sancte Míchaël,
Dux et præpósite cæléstium exercítuum,
Custos animárum,
Dómitor spirítuum rebéllum,
Serve in domu Regis Divíni,
et condúctor mirábilis noster,
Qui cum excelléntia
   et virtúte cælésti fulges,

Salutation VIII

By the intercession of Saint Michael
and the Celestial choir of Archangels,
may the Lord give us perseverance in faith
   and in good works,
in order that we gain the glory of Paradise. Amen.

Our Father… Three times: Hail Mary…

Salutation IX

By the intercession of Saint Michael
and the Celestial choir of Angels,
may the Lord grant us to be protected by them
   in this mortal life
and conducted hereafter to eternal glory. Amen.

Our Father… Three times: Hail Mary…

Conclusion

In honour of Michael: Our Father…

In honour of Gabriel: Our Father…

In honour of Raphael: Our Father…

In honour of the guardian angel: Our Father…

Antiphon

O glorious Prince Saint Michael,
chief and commander of the heavenly hosts,
guardian of souls,
vanquisher of rebel spirits,
servant in the house of the Divine King,
and our admirable conductor,
thou who dost shine with excellence
   and superhuman virtue,

liberáre nos a malo digenéris,
Qui ad te tornámus cum confidéntiæ,
et propítio præsídio tuo
da nobis Deum magis fidéliter quotídie servíre.

℣. Ora pro nobis, O Glorióse Sancte Míchaël,
Princeps Ecclésiæ Iesus Christi.

℟. Ut digni efficiámur promissiónibus eius.

ORATIO AD CONCLUSIONEM

Omnípotens Ætérne Deus,
qui prodígio bonitátis
et cleménte volens salve omnes hómines,
gloriosíssimum Archángelum Sanctum Míchaël,
   Príncipem Ecclésia Tua constituísti,
fac nos dignos, te rogámus,
liberári eius præssídio poténte
ab adversáriis cunctis,
ne nos vexent,
   in hora mortis nostræ,
sed nos perdúcti simus
ab eo in præséntiam augústam divínæ maiestátis tuæ.
Hoc orémus méritis Iesus Christi,
   Dómini nostri. ℟. Amen.

vouchsafe to deliver us from all evil,
who turn to thee with confidence,
and enable us by thy gracious protection
to serve God more and more faithfully every day.

℣. Pray for us, O Glorious Saint Michael,
Prince of the Church of Jesus Christ.

℟. That we may be made worthy of His promises.

CONCLUDING PRAYER

Almighty and everlasting God,
who by a prodigy of Goodness
and a merciful desire for the salvation of all men,
has appointed the most glorious Archangel
   Saint Michael, Prince of Thy Church,
make us worthy, we beseech Thee,
to be delivered by his powerful protection
from all our enemies,
that none of them may harass us
   at the hour of our death,
but that we may be conducted by him
into the august presence of Thy Divine Majesty.
This we beg through the merits of Jesus Christ
   our Lord. ℟. Amen.

Orationes variæ

HYMNUS

Te splendor et virtus Patris,
Te vita, Iesu, córdium,
Ab ore qui pendent tuo,
Laudámus inter Angelos.

Tibi mille densa míllium
Ducum coróna mílitat;
Sed éxplicat victor Crucem
Míchaël salútis Sígnifer.

Dracónis hic dirum caput
In ima pellit tártara,
Ducémque cum rebéllibus
Cælésti ab arce fúlminat.

Contra ducem supérbiæ
Sequámur hunc nos Príncipem,
Ut detur ex Agni throno
Nobis coróna glóriæ.

Patri simúlque Fílio,
Tibíque, Sancte Spíritus,
Sicut fuit, sit iúgiter
Sǽculum per omne glória. Amen.

ANTIPHONA

Princeps gloriosíssime, Míchaël Archángele,
esto memor nostri;
hic et ubíque
semper precáre pro nobis Fílium Dei.

Various Prayers (Orationes variæ)

Various Prayers

HYMN

O Jesus! life-spring of the soul!
The Father's Power and Glory bright!
Thee with the Angels we extol;
From Thee they draw their life and light.

Thy thousand, thousand hosts are spread,
Embattled o'er the azure sky;
But Michael bears Thy standard dread,
And lifts the mighty Cross on high.

He in that sign the rebel powers
Did with their dragon prince expel:
And hurled them from the heaven's high towers,
Down like a thunderbolt to hell.

Grant us with Michael still, O Lord,
Against the Prince of pride to fight;
So may a crown be our reward,
Before the Lamb's pure throne of light.

To God the Father and the Son
And Holy Paraclete to Thee,
As evermore hath been before,
Be glory through eternity. Amen.

[tr. E. Caswall]

ANTIPHON

Most glorious Prince, Michael the Archangel,
be ever mindful of us;
here and everywhere
pray always for us to the Son of God.

℣. In conspéctu Angelórum psallam tibi,
Deus meus.

℟. Adorábo ad templum sanctum tuum,
et confitébor nómini tuo.

[*Psalmus* 138 (137), 1b-2]

Deus,
qui miro órdine Angelórum
ministéria hominúmque dispénsas,
concéde propítius,
ut a quibus tibi ministrántibus in cælo semper assístitur,
ab his in terra vita nostra muniátur.
Per Christum Dóminum nostrum. Amen.

Oratio ad Sanctum Michael Archangelorum

Sancte Míchaël Archángele, defénde nos in prœlio,
contra nequítiam
et insídias diáboli esto præsídium.
Imperet illi Deus, súpplices deprecámur:
tuque, Princeps milítiæ cæléstis,
Sátanam aliósque spíritus malígnos,
qui ad perditiónem animárum pervagántur in mundo,
divína virtúte, in inférnum detrúde. Amen.

[Leo pp. XIII, 1884]

Invocatio

Sancte Míchael Archángele,
defénde nos in prǽlio,
ut non pereámus in treméndo iudício.

Various Prayers (*Orationes variæ*)

℣. Before the Angels I will sing praise unto Thee,
O my God.

℟. I will worship at Thy holy temple,
and praise Thy name.

[*Psalm* 137:2]

O God,
who in wondrous order dost ordain and constitute
the services of men and Angels;
mercifully grant
that our life may be defended on earth
by them that stand near Thee,
evermore ministering to Thee in heaven.
Through Christ our Lord. Amen.

[*The Raccolta*, 444]

PRAYER TO SAINT MICHAEL THE ARCHANGEL

Saint Michael the Archangel, defend us in battle;
be our defense
against the wickedness and snares of the devil.
May God rebuke him, we humbly pray.
And do you, O prince of the heavenly host,
by the power of God thrust into hell Satan
and all the evil spirits
who prowl about the world for the ruin of souls. Amen.

[Pope Leo XIII, 1884; *The Raccolta*, 447]

INVOCATION

Saint Michael the Archangel,
defend us in the battle,
that we perish not in the fearful judgment.

Oratio ad Angelum Custodem

Ángele Dei, qui custos es mei,
me tibi commíssum pietáte supérna hódie
(vel hac nocte),
illúmina, custódi, rege et gubérna. Amen.

Altera Oratio

O sancte ángele Dei,
minister cæléstis impérii,
cui Deus omnípotens mei custódiam deputávi:
per maiestátem eius et pietátem
te humíliter déprecor,
ut custódias ánimam meam et corpus meum:
et omnes sensus meos a pravis et illícitis desidériis:
a nóxiis, vanis,
et immúndis cogitatiónibus,
et ab illusiónibus malignorum spirítuum:
a pollutióne mentis et córporis:
et ab insídiis inimicórum meórum visibílium
et invisibílium quæréntium ánimam meam:
et sis mihi protéctor tutus, ubicúmque íero
diébus ac nóctibus,
horis atque moméntis,
et consérva me in mundo ópere:
et confírma me in timóre et amóre Iesu Christi
cum sanctis desidériis:
et post hanc míseram et caducam vitam
perduc ánimam meam ad ætérnam felicitátem:
ubi cum Deo et ómnibus sanctis
gáudeat sine fine:
præstánte Dómino nostro Iesu Christo:
cui est honor et glória in sæculórum sǽcula.
Amen.

[*Sarum Horae*; cf. *Monumenta Ritualia*]

Various Prayers (*Orationes variæ*)

Prayer to the Guardian Angel

Angel of God, my guardian dear,
to whom His love commits me here;
ever this day (or night) be at my side,
to light and guard, to rule and guide. Amen.

[*The Raccolta*, 452]

Another Prayer

O holy angel of God,
minister of heavenly power,
whom almighty God appointed as my guardian,
through His majesty and devotion
I humbly beg thee to guard my body, soul,
and all my senses
from perverse and illicit desires,
from hurtful, vain,
and impure thoughts,
from the illusions of evil spirits,
from the pollution of mind and body,
and from the snares of my visible
and invisible enemies seeking my soul.
Be my watchful protector wherever I may go,
night and day,
every hour and every moment,
and preserve me in clean works.
Strengthen me with holy desires
in the fear and love of Jesus Christ.
And after this wretched and perishable life,
lead my soul to eternal happiness;
where with God and all His saints
it may rejoice without end;
especially with our Lord Jesus Christ:
to whom be honour and glory for ever and ever.
Amen.

Oratio ad Sanctum Gabriel Archangelorum

O fortitúdo Dei, sancte Gábriël,
qui vírgini Maríæ incarnatiónem
Unigéniti Fílii Dei annuntiásti,
laudo et véneror te, o elécte Spíritus,
et supplex oro,
ut meus apud Iesum Christum, Salvatórem nostrum,
et eius benedíctam matrem
advocátus esse,
atque in ómnibus angústiis me solári
et corroboráre velis,
ne ullis unquam tentatiónibus superátus,
Deum meum peccáto offéndam. Amen.

[P. Gaudentius, *Orate Fratres* (Herder, 1901)]

Oratio ad Sanctum Raphael Archangelorum

O cæléstis médice et comes fidelíssime,
sancte Ráphaël,
qui Tobíæ senióri visum restituísti,
iuniórem per omnes suscépti itíneris
vias deduxísti
et incólumem conservásti:
esto córporis et ánimæ meæ médicus,
pelle ignorántiæ tenébras,
mihíque in periculósa huius
vitæ peregrinatióne constánter assíste,
donec me ad cæléstem pátriam perdúcas. Amen.

[P. Gaudentius, *Orate Fratres* (Herder, 1901)]

Various Prayers (Orationes variæ)

Prayer to Saint Gabriel the Archangel

O strength of God, Saint Gabriel,
you who announced to the Virgin Mary
the incarnation of the only-begotten Son of God,
I praise thee and honor thee, O elect spirit.
I humbly beg thee,
with Jesus Christ our Saviour
and with His Blessed Mother,
to be my advocate.
I also pray that you would comfort me
and strengthen me in all my difficulties,
lest at any time I may be overcome by temptation
and I might offend God by sinning. Amen.

Prayer to Saint Raphael the Archangel

O heavenly doctor and most faithful companion,
Saint Raphael,
you who restored sight to the elder Tobit,
and escorted the younger Tobias
throughout his appointed journey
and kept him safe and sound,
be the doctor of my body and soul.
Dispel the darkness of my ignorance,
and assist me in the dangerous journey
of this life always,
until you lead me to my heavenly homeland. Amen.

Hymnus

Christe, sanctórum decus Angelórum,
Gentis humánæ Sator et Redémptor,
Caélitum nobis tríbuas beátas
Scándere sedes.

Angelus pacis Míchaël in ædes
Caélitus nostras véniat, serénæ
Auctor ut pacis lacrimósa in orcum
Bella reléget.

Angelus fortis Gábriël, ut hostes
Pellat antíquos, et amíca cælo,
Quæ triumphátor státuit per orbem,
Templa revísat.

Angelus nostræ médicus salútis,
Adsit e cælo Ráphaël, ut omnes
Sanet ægrótos, dubiósque vitæ
Dírigat actus.

Virgo dux pacis Genetríxque lucis,
Et sacer nobis chorus Angelórum
Semper assístat, simul et micántis
Régia cæli.

Præstet hoc nobis Déitas beáta
Patris, ac Nati, paritérque Sancti
Spíritus, cuius résonat per omnem
Glória mundum. Amen.

[*Breviarium Romanum*, editio typica 1961,
In Dedicatione S. Míchaëlis Archangeli]

Various Prayers (*Orationes variæ*)

Hymn

Christ, of the Angels praise and adoration,
Father and Saviour thou, of every nation,
Graciously grant us all to gain a station,
Where thou art reigning.

Angel all peaceful, to our dwellings, send us,
Michael, from heaven coming to befriend us,
Breathing serenest peace may he attend us,
Grim war dispelling.

Angel of strength, who triumphed, tumults quelling,
Gabriel send us, ancient foes expelling,
Oft in these temples may he make his dwelling,
Dear unto heaven.

Angel Physician, health on man bestowing,
Raphael send us from the skies all glowing,
All sickness curing, wisest counsel showing
In doubt and danger.

May the fair Mother of the Light be o'er us,
Virgin of peace, with all the Angel chorus,
And may the heavenly army go before us,
Guiding and guarding.

O May the Godhead, endless bliss possessing,
Father, Son, Spirit, grant to us this blessing;
All this creation joins his praise confessing,
Now and forever. Amen.

[*The Roman Breviary*
(Benziger Brothers, Inc., 1964), pp. 1067-1068]

Domina Nostra Publishing

P.O. Box 1464
Monterey, CA. 93942-1464
USA

info@DominaNostraPublishing.com
www.DominaNostraPublishing.com

www.ingramcontent.com/pod-product-compliance
Lightning Source LLC
Chambersburg PA
CBHW062107290426
44110CB00022B/2735